Space Telescope

Space Telescope

by Franklyn M. Branley

Illustrated by Giulio Maestro

A Voyage Into Space Book

Thomas Y. Crowell / New York

All photographs, except those on pages 2, 3, and 47
courtesy of NASA. Pages 2 and 3:
Courtesy Yerkes Observatory;
page 47: Courtesy Hale Observatory.

Space Telescope
Text copyright © 1985 by Franklin M. Branley
Illustrations copyright © 1985 by Guilio Maestro
For information address
Thomas Y. Crowell Junior Books, 10 East 53rd Street,
New York, N.Y. 10022. Published simultaneously in
Canada by Fitzhenry & Whiteside Limited, Toronto.

Library of Congress Cataloging in Publication Data
Branley, Franklyn Mansfield, 1915–
  Space telescope.

  (A Voyage into space book)
  Summary: Describes the telescope which will soon
be placed in orbit around the Earth to take pictures
from space, compares it to other kinds of telescopes,
and discusses how its discoveries could extend man's
exploration of the universe.
  1. Space telescope—Juvenile literature. [1. Space
telescope. 2. Telescope. 3. Outer space—Exploration]
I. Maestro, Guilio, ill. II. Title. III. Series.
QB88.B76 1985   522'.2   84-45341
ISBN 0-690-04433-X
ISBN 0-690-04434-8 (lib. bdg.)

Designed by Al Cetta
1 2 3 4 5 6 7 8 9 10
First Edition

Contents

Space Telescope peers farther into space than any
Earth-based instrument.

1. About Telescopes

In 1986 the most powerful telescope in the world, or out of it, will be carried into space by a space shuttle. It will be called Space Telescope. It will operate during the remaining years of this century, and will still be working in the twenty-first century. The telescope may tell us more about the stars and the universe than we have learned during the thousands of years since ancient astronomers first gazed into the sky.

Early astronomers had no telescopes to help them. Telescopes were not invented until the early seventeenth century. In 1610 Galileo, the Italian astronomer, became the first person to look into the sky through a telescope. He was the first to see dark spots on the sun, craters on the moon, four large satellites of Jupiter, and bulges (later found to be

Galileo Galilei was the first person to gaze into the sky through a telescope. Here he presents his telescope to the council of officials.

rings) on either side of Saturn. Everywhere he looked, Galileo made discoveries with his fabulous telescope.

When Space Telescope is turned on, it may also make discoveries wherever it looks. The telescope may see planets out beyond our solar system, going around distant stars. This would be solid proof that there really are planets way

Two of Galileo's "optic tubes." Crude as they were,
Galileo made many discoveries with them.

out beyond Neptune and Pluto. It's something many people
have suspected for a long time. Where there are planets,
there may also be life. Space Telescope may give us clues to
where we should search for life beyond Earth. It may find
that Earth people are not alone in the universe.

Space Telescope will be carried from Earth aboard a space
shuttle. It is just the right size to fit easily into the cargo bay

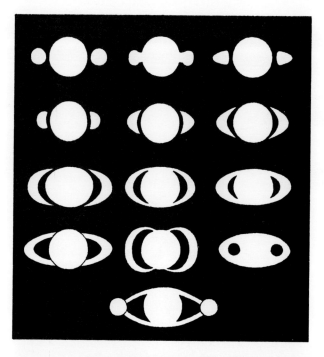

Some drawings of Saturn made in the early 1600s by several different observers. Across the top are versions seen by Galileo. After his first discovery, the "ears" of Saturn were seen to be more like a ring formation.

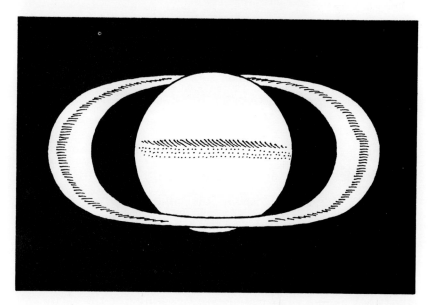

of the orbiter—that's the part of a shuttle that goes into orbit around Earth.

The orbiter will carry Space Telescope to an altitude of 600 kilometers (375 miles). The telescope will be lifted out of the cargo bay and released. The orbiter will then return to Earth. Space Telescope will not; it will be in its own orbit, and it will remain in space for years, probably into the twenty-first century. No astronomers will ever look through Space Telescope. It will take pictures of what it sees, and will send those pictures to Earth.

Space Telescope may see objects as they were some 13 to 15 billion years ago, long before Earth and the sun were created. Astronomers have long hoped to learn about events that occurred that long ago. But they have not been able to do so because their telescopes have not been powerful enough. Also, for the most part, their telescopes have been land based—they have stayed right here on Earth. That means they have had to contend with several problems.

Limits of Telescopes

Telescopes on Earth are at the bottom of an ocean of air. Light or any other form of energy from the sun, stars, and planets must go through the air to reach earth telescopes. And that's the problem. Only a small part of the energy can get through the atmosphere.

Space Telescope will see Saturn looking like this photograph made by a Voyager planet probe. The telescope will see the whole planet this clearly, and will be able to observe it for hours. You can see shadows of the rings, as well as Tethys (above) and Dione (below), two of Saturn's many satellites.

When most of us think about telescopes, we have in mind the kind we look through: telescopes that gather in light energy, or optical telescopes, as they are called. But the sun and other stars also give off other kinds of energy. For example, they release radio waves and infrared radiation.

Astronomers strive to "see" an object in space in as many ways as possible. They are able to see the sun in visible light, the way you and I see it. But they can also "see" the sun by its radio waves, its heat waves, and its ultraviolet and X rays. In order to pick up these waves, special kinds of telescopes are needed.

Radio waves are picked up by receivers called radio telescopes, which enable scientists to "see" a radio sun, for example. This shows the locations on the sun that produce radio waves. Infrared radiation is heat energy that is given off by anything that is warm. Infrared telescopes in satellites are able to pick up that radiation. Other telescopes are able to receive ultraviolet rays and X rays.

But astronomers cannot receive all these kinds of energy at Earth's surface because of the air blanket that surrounds Earth. The drawing on page 8 shows the many kinds of energy. Notice that there are "windows" in the air blanket permitting only parts of the energy to reach Earth's surface, and so providing a limited view of the universe. As you can see, the windows allow only visible light and certain radio waves to come through.

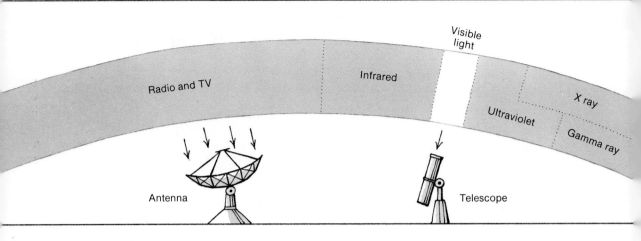

Radio and TV

Infrared

Visible light

Ultraviolet

X ray

Gamma ray

Antenna

Telescope

All kinds of radiation together comprise the electromagnetic spectrum—radio waves, infrared, visible light, ultraviolet, X rays, gamma rays. Because of the atmosphere, instruments on Earth can detect only light and radio waves.

Space Telescope will be far enough above the dense atmosphere for it to be able to see a lot more of the ultraviolet and also the infrared light. As you can see from the drawing on page 9, it will be able to pick up a lot more energy than even the big 5-meter (200-inch) telescope on Mount Palomar in California.

Also, Space Telescope will have perfect seeing conditions. On Earth, telescopes can be operated only about half the nights in a year, when there are "good seeing" conditions. "Good seeing" means there is no dust, smog, clouds, or pollu-

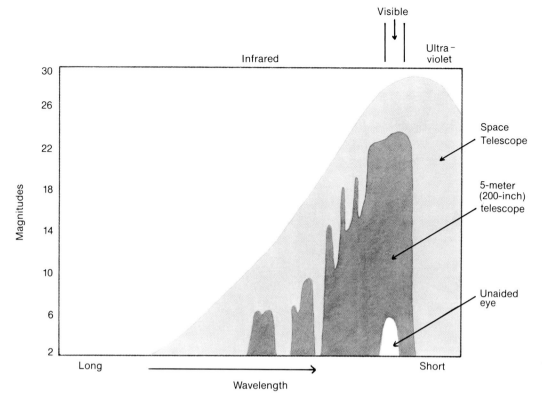

Space Telescope will eventually be able to pick up radiation from the far infrared to the far ultraviolet—much more than the 5-meter (200-inch) Hale telescope. The human eye can perceive only a limited range of wavelengths—those that make visible light.

tants of any kind. There are not large temperature variations in the air. Also, the atmosphere is not lighted by the moon or by lights from cities and traffic. Because Earth-based telescopes are at the bottom of the air ocean, it is rare to have perfect seeing conditions. Images of stars and other objects are often not sharp and clear. They are more apt to be dim and blurry, and so of limited value. In space there is no atmosphere; no smog, clouds, or city lights. Space Telescope will have perfect seeing. Images will be sharp.

In space there is no scintillation—that's the technical word for the stars' twinkling. Even when seeing conditions are ideal, stars twinkle when they are viewed from Earth. It's because the atmosphere is made of layers much like the layers of a cake, each layer having a different temperature and each in motion. As starlight comes through the layers, it is bent a bit, so it does not look steady. The starlight's path wobbles, or twinkles, making images somewhat blurry.

Space Telescope will look into a sky that is completely black. And it will always be black, just as the sky is when seen from the moon. Our sky has brightness and color only because water droplets and molecules in the atmosphere are lit by the sun. If Earth had no atmosphere, our sky would be continually black as night.

The stars that Space Telescope sees will shine with steady brilliance in a jet-black sky.

Telescopes: Reflectors and Refractors

There are two main types of optical telescopes: reflectors, which reflect light from a mirror; and refractors, which bend light with a lens. Both are designed to collect light over a large area and then concentrate it into a small image.

Galileo's refractor

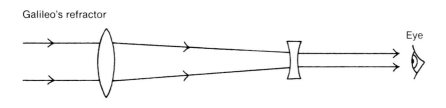

Eye

A modern refractor

A Cassegrain reflector

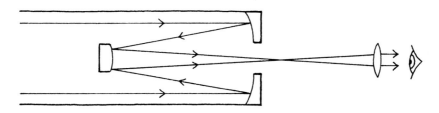

Refractor telescopes use lenses to collect light. The earliest telescopes were refractors.

Reflecting telescopes use mirrors to collect light. Space Telescope is a reflector.

Space Telescope is a reflector.

Galileo's telescope was a refractor. A lens at the end of the tube gathered light and formed an image of the object—the moon, for example. Another lens enlarged the image seen by the eye.

Lenses and mirrors are effective because they can gather in more light than our eyes can. The amount of light we can collect is limited by the size of the pupil, or opening, of our eyes, which is about a quarter inch across—much less when the light is bright. If we could enlarge the pupil, we'd receive more light. That's what a telescope does. Galileo's telescope had a collecting lens 4.5 centimeters (1.75 inches) across. Space Telescope will have a collecting mirror 2.4 meters (94.5 inches) across.

A light gatherer of this size must be a mirror rather than a lens. For a lens to be useful, it must be perfect throughout. There must not be the slightest flaw in the glass. It is just about impossible to make a chunk of glass any larger than 1.5 meters (60 inches) across and keep it absolutely perfect. Even if it could be done, the lens would have to be very heavy, and therefore it would be difficult to support in a telescope tube. One and a half meters seems to be the limit for a refracting telescope.

A large instrument such as Space Telescope uses a mirror for another reason. Lenses produce color fringes or halos. An image of the moon, for example, would have dim bands of color around it. That's what happened with Galileo's telescope.

It's because light is made of many colors—red, orange, yellow, green, blue, violet—all mixed together. Each color is a different wavelength. A lens bends violet and blue light

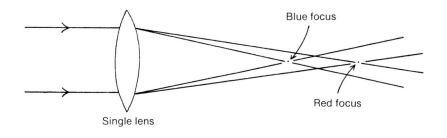

Single lens

Blue focus

Red focus

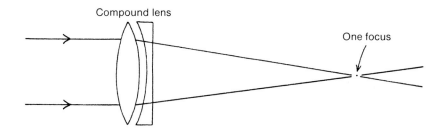

Compound lens

One focus

A lens refracts light. Short (blue) waves are bent more than long (red) waves. The colors are spread, making color fringes around an image. This blurring of the edges of an image is corrected by using a compound lens, one that is made of two or more different kinds of glass.

(the shorter waves) more than it does red light (the longer waves). Each color is separated from the others. The effect is to spread the light into a band of colors, a halo around an image.

A mirror does not do this. It reflects light. The mirror is curved. Whatever light falls on the mirror is reflected. Each light beam is turned slightly so that all the light is concentrated into a small image. In Space Telescope, this concentrated light falls on another, much smaller mirror. From that mirror the light goes to a camera, or to some other instrument, where it is recorded.

Space Telescope is a special kind of reflector called Cassegrain. It is named after Guillaume Cassegrain, the Frenchman who in the seventeenth century invented such an arrangement of mirrors. Light enters Space Telescope and travels to the end of the tube, where it strikes the main, or primary, mirror. That mirror reflects a concentrated beam of light back to a smaller, or secondary, mirror. This mirror concentrates the light further, making it into a narrow and intense beam. The light reflects from that mirror through a

The primary, or main, mirror of Space Telescope collects light. The light is reflected to the secondary mirror, and from there it goes to the focal plane.

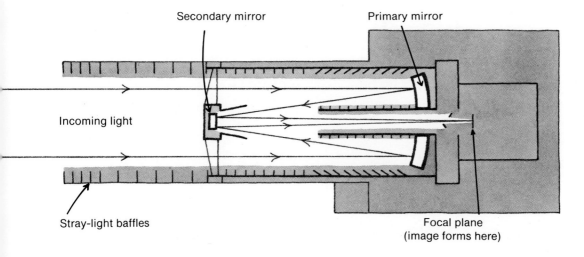

Secondary mirror   Primary mirror

Incoming light

Stray-light baffles

Focal plane
(image forms here)

60-centimeter (2-foot) hole in the center of the large mirror. It is brought to a tight focus just behind the mirror.

We'll continue to trace the journey of the light in just a moment. First, let's consider other aspects of telescopes so we can see why Space Telescope is so impressive.

Telescope Power

Galileo's telescope was 32 power. That's about the rating of the type of telescope that can now be bought in a novelty store. It makes objects appear 32 times closer. Binoculars rated 7×35 have a magnifying power of 7; objects appear 7 times closer.

The greater the power, the dimmer the image. Generally, the greatest power for a telescope is 100 times the diameter in inches of the light collector. So the limit of a 6-inch (15-centimeter) telescope would be 600. Practically, this does not usually work out. The maximum is closer to 50 times the diameter of the lens or mirror, making it 300 for a 6-inch instrument. The power of a telescope can be changed by changing the viewing lens. It is not a very important measure of a telescope. Of much more value is what is called "resolving power."

This is the ability of a telescope to separate two objects. For example, two stars may appear so close together that their light blends, and a small telescope sees only one single

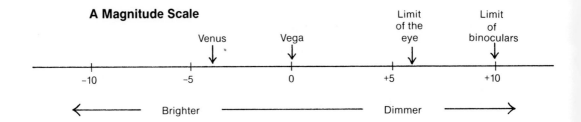

A Magnitude Scale

		Venus	Vega		Limit of the eye	Limit of binoculars

−10   −5   0   +5   +10

← ——— Brighter ——————————— Dimmer ——— →

Magnitude Range and Limits

Sun	−26.5	Proxima Centauri	+10.7
Full Moon	−12.5	Small telescope	+13
Venus	−4	5-meter (200-inch) telescope	+23
Jupiter	−2	Space Telescope	+28
Polaris (North Star)	+2		

Magnitude is a measure of brightness of stars and other objects. The larger the number, the dimmer the object. The Sun, brightest of all objects, has a magnitude of −26.5.

image. A telescope with high resolving power is able to see each image separately. The resolving power of Space Telescope is much greater than that of Earth-based instruments. The telescope will be able to pick out stars that have not yet been seen as separate images. It will observe more stars and see them more clearly.

Magnitude

Another way of rating a telescope is by the faintest objects it can see. Brightness is measured by giving the magnitude of a star. Before there were instruments to measure the brightness of stars, people could only estimate brightness. The brigntest stars they could see were called first magnitude, or first in importance. The dimmest they could see were sixth magnitude. The other stars were somewhere between. Later, when there were instruments to measure brightness and there were telescopes that could see dim objects, the scale was extended. Very bright stars, and objects such as the sun and moon, were given minus numbers. For example, the magnitude of the sun is –26. Very dim objects were given larger and larger magnitudes. A 10-centimeter (4-inch) telescope can pick up stars of 12th magnitude, a 25-centimeter (10-inch) one can detect to 14th magnitude, and so on. Very large telescopes, such as the 5-meter (200-inch) in California and the 6-meter (236-inch) in Russia, can see to magnitude 25 or thereabouts. Space Telescope will produce sharp images, and it is expected to see objects 50 times dimmer than the faintest ones visible with Earth-based telescopes.

2. Space Telescope

Space Telescope is not the largest telescope ever built. There are several much larger, and there are two giants—the 5-meter (200-inch) Hale telescope on Mount Palomar, and the 6-meter (236-inch) telescope in the Soviet Union. But these telescopes are land based, so they are hampered by Earth's atmosphere. For example, the 200-inch instrument can see clearly features on the moon that are only some 1,000 meters (3,300 feet) across. That's about eleven times the length of a football field. So the telescope can see plains and mountains

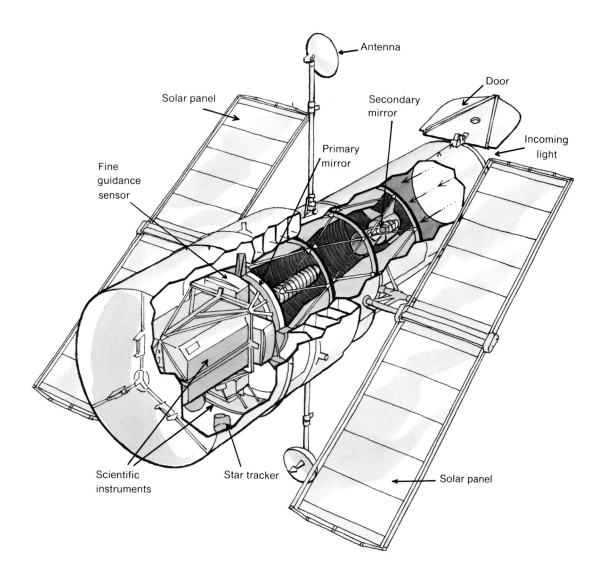

Antenna

Door

Solar panel

Secondary
mirror

Incoming
light

Fine
guidance
sensor

Primary
mirror

Scientific
instruments

Star tracker

Solar panel

A cross section of Space Telescope. Parts are built in
modules, making it easier to repair equipment while the
craft is in orbit.

only if they are that large—it cannot see smaller details. If the telescope were in space, however, it could identify features that were only 30 meters (100 feet) across, a third the size of a football field.

Space Telescope is much smaller than those great instruments—2.4 meters (94.5 inches) across. But remember, it will be outside the atmosphere, and it will be able to keep looking at an object for several hours. As mentioned in the previous chapter, Space Telescope is designed to detect objects fifty times dimmer than those that we have yet seen. Also, it is expected to see objects as much as seven times farther away. Another big advantage is that Space Telescope can be used many more hours every day than Earth-based instruments, which are not useful during daylight hours.

The Spacecraft

The picture on page 19 shows a side view of Space Telescope. The parts that are most apparent are the two flat solar panels and the tube itself. Notice that the base of the tube has the greater diameter. This is the section that contains scientific instruments as well as support systems, both of which we'll discuss further on in this chapter.

When it is launched from Cape Canaveral in Florida, Space

Space Telescope in orbit some 600 kilometers (375 miles) above Earth.

Telescope will weigh a total of 12,900 kilograms (28,380 pounds), about 14 tons. It will be a little over 13 meters (43 feet) long, and 4.27 meters (14 feet) across.

Electric power for the instruments and transmitters of the telescope is generated by solar cells mounted on large panels. At launch the panels are folded together and packed tightly into canisters only 30 centimeters (1 foot) across. Once in orbit, the folded panels are released from the canisters. They expand to 2.3 meters (7.6 feet) wide and 11.8 meters (39 feet) long. During the interval when sunlight falls on the panels, the cells will recharge six batteries. The batteries will furnish at least 2,400 watts of power, an ample supply for all the equipment aboard.

During launch a door covers the end of the tube. When the door is opened, it remains fast to the tube so it may deflect stray light that might come from the moon, the sun, and Earth. Inside the tube there are baffles that also catch stray light, preventing it from reaching the main mirror. The path of light through the tube is shown in the diagram on page 14. The drawing does not show how complicated the structure really is. You can see that more clearly in the pictures on pages 19 and 23. One picture shows the lower section of the tube, the part that contains the two mirrors and the scientific instruments. The other picture shows how this section fits into the forward shell.

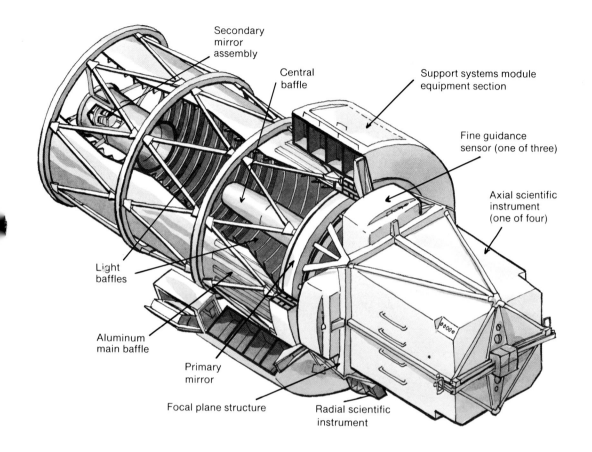

Secondary
mirror
assembly

Central
baffle

Support systems module
equipment section

Fine guidance
sensor (one of three)

Axial scientific
instrument
(one of four)

Light
baffles

Aluminum
main baffle

Primary
mirror

Focal plane structure

Radial scientific
instrument

Details of Space Telescope. Notice especially the light
baffles, support system, and scientific-instrument
package.

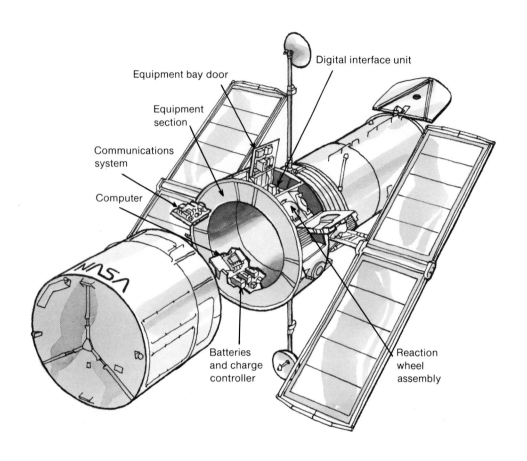

Equipment bay door

Equipment
section

Communications
system

Computer

Digital interface unit

Batteries
and charge
controller

Reaction
wheel
assembly

Another view of Space Telescope, showing modules in
the ring of support equipment.

Notice the handrails and access doors. They are needed for maintenance work. Space Telescope is designed so it can be repaired in space. If instruments do not work properly, or if new and better ones are developed after launch, they can be repaired or replaced.

During a typical maintenance operation, a shuttle orbiter will move in close to the telescope and will match its orbit and velocity to that of the telescope. When the two orbits match exactly, the cargo arm will be extended to the telescope and made fast. The arm will then gently maneuver the telescope into the cargo area of the orbiter, where it will be held upright. Astronauts in space suits will then leave the command section of the orbiter and proceed to the telescope. They will swing open a door in the base of the tube so they can reach the faulty equipment. The fault may lie in one of the instruments. Like all the equipment of the telescope, each instrument is built in modules, or sections, that snap together. Trouble may be corrected by replacing a module rather than the entire instrument. Each module is connected and wired using simple snap devices. All the astronaut does is snap out the old module and snap in a new one. That way, all parts of the telescope can be kept in top working condition, and can be improved as new and better instruments are developed.

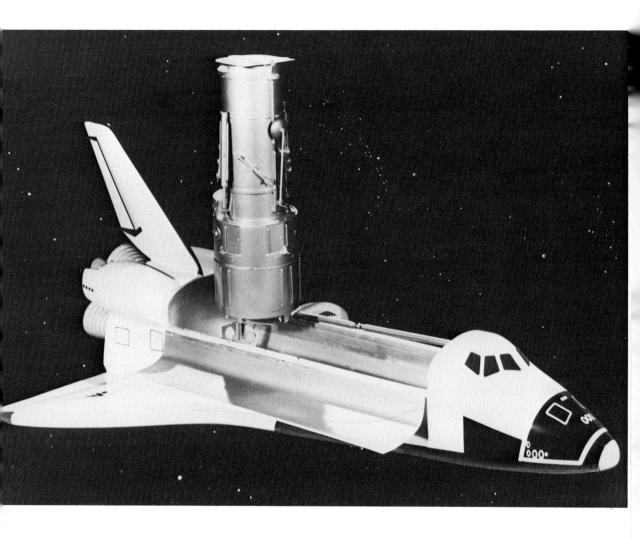

During maintenance, Space Telescope will be brought aboard orbiter and held in upright position.

Astronauts will work outside the orbiter, changing modules and making repairs as needed.

The Main, or Primary, Mirror

The main part of Space Telescope, the large mirror, is 2.4 meters (94.5 inches) in diameter and weighs 829 kilograms (1,823 pounds). The mirror began as a large disk of titanium silicate glass 32.5 centimers (12.5 inches) thick and weighing 1,090 kilograms (2,400 pounds). This kind of glass expands and contracts very little with changes in temperature. Sections of the back of the disk are hollowed out so that it looks like a honeycomb. This reduces weight and makes the structure less rigid than if it were completely solid.

The top surface is a glass disk fused to the honeycomb base. At the start it was 3.7 centimeters (1.5 inches) thick. After two years of grinding, the top surface was reduced to 2.5 centimeters (1 inch) and shaped into a smooth curve. Then it was polished and tested over and over again. Finally the curvature was perfectly smooth and even. It is so perfect that if the mirror were the size of the United States, no hill or valley would be more than 5 centimeters (2 inches) above or below the surface of it.

After the glass was ground and polished, it was coated with a thin metal surface to reflect more light.

The heart of Space Telescope is the main mirror,
which has been ground to a very accurate curve, polished,
and coated with metal.

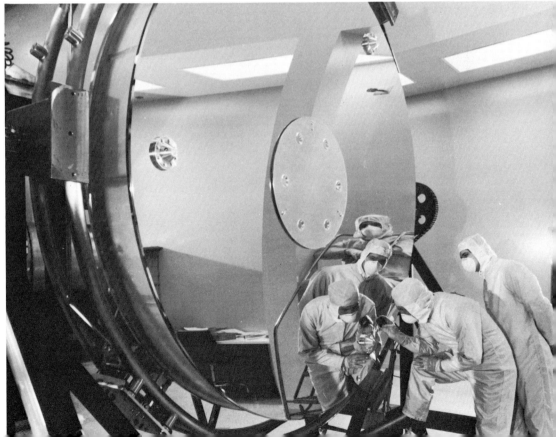

Other Parts of Space Telescope

Space Telescope will work only when all its parts are operating properly. It needs electric power, light baffles, sensitive computers—and ingenious engineering. There are many parts. They can be grouped into three systems. The first system is the optics, which consist of two mirrors: the large one that collects light, and the small, secondary mirror that reflects the light to the instruments. A second system is made of the scientific instruments, discussed in the next section. The third is made of those devices that make it all work—the support system. The support system consists of the power supply: the solar panels and batteries; radios to communicate with a relay satellite and through that satellite with Earth stations; temperature regulation; and pointing and control devices for pointing the telescope exactly on target and controlling the position with great accuracy over long periods of time. Some of the objects that astronomers are seeking will be so dim, even to Space Telescope, that exposures of 10 to 12 hours will be needed to gather enough light to produce a clear image. During the entire exposure, the telescope must be kept steady. It must not waver at all, otherwise the image would be blurred and so not useful.

Part of the support system is the door at the end of the tube. It protects the optics against sudden flashes of light that might come from the sun. These would spoil the observation being made. Also, the heat could cause the mirror to expand and so damage it. To be sure that does not happen, the telescope will always be turned away from the sun. This means it will not be able to see Mercury at all, for the planet is always close to the Sun. Venus will not be seen well either, for the same reason.

The tube door is only one of many baffles. The most essential one is just in front of the primary mirror, as you can see in the diagram on page 23. This central baffle is a narrow tube that allows only light from the secondary mirror to pass to the focus of the telescope.

Just in front of the main mirror is a ring that contains support-system equipment. The batteries are placed in a cooler section of the ring, the part that will be turned away from the sun. Reaction wheels that work like gyroscopes are also in the ring. Once a gyroscope—or any wheel—is spinning, it tends to hold its position. This is why a bike is steady once it is rolling. The spin of the gyros affects the entire telescope, tending to hold it steady. The telescope is further stabilized by using Earth's magnetic field. The field serves as a steady reference for metal rods that are controlled by an onboard computer.

Optical sensors work with the gyros to point and hold the telescope to a target. The sensors are devices that point at reference stars and lock onto them, holding the telescope in position for hour after hour if necessary. The slightest movement away from the guide stars is fed into a computer that modifies the gyros to bring the telescope back into line. This equipment is so accurate that it can hold the telescope almost exactly on target. It is like sending a beam of light from Washington to Boston and hitting a dime at its exact center. The equipment can hold to this accuracy for ten hours or more.

Should an astronomer wish to change the telescope's position, a radio signal is relayed to a computer that regulates control motors that can slowly swing the telescope through 90 degrees or so, and lock it onto another target.

In outer space there are wide extremes of temperature. The surfaces of an object exposed to sunlight become very hot, for there is no atmosphere to filter and dilute the light. At the same time the opposite sides of the same object will be extremely cold, since no solar radiation reaches them. The temperature difference between one side and the other is often 200 to 275 degrees Celsius (400 to 500 degrees Fahrenheit).

The mirrors and scientific instruments can adjust to moderate swings in temperature. But extreme changes could cause the mirrors to bend slightly and so make them unusable, and could also cause a breakdown of the instruments. Therefore Space Telescope has built-in heat controls. The outside and the inside are coated with thermal (heat-resistant) materials. Vital parts of the instruments are well insulated to save heat. Also, several electric heaters maintain a steady temperature in instruments that require it.

When radio commands for altering the operation of Space Telescope are sent from Earth, they go to a central computer, or nerve center. The computer then directs the command to the proper part of the telescope. That might be the pointer controls, a scientific instrument, or the communications system.

A smaller computer has control of the instruments. This computer also receives data from the instruments, records the information, and gets it ready for transmission to Earth.

Another computer takes care of the power needs. It monitors the generation of electricity by the solar cells, the storage of electricity in the batteries, and the control and distribution of electricity within the spacecraft. It sorts out the electricity needed for operation, and delivers to the various parts of the telescope the amounts required.

Science Instruments

There is no "eyepiece" on Space Telescope, for no one will ever look through it. Energy gathered by the telescope is directed to five science instruments located at the base of the main tube. Light gathered by the big mirror is directed to the small mirror. From there the light goes to the instruments.

Signals from Earth direct the light to one or another of the instruments for study and analysis. Each instrument operates independently, and so it can be removed at a later time or replaced without affecting any of the other instruments.

Two of the instruments are specialized cameras; one has a wide field and will be used to look at broad areas of the sky. The other will detect very faint objects and will look for details in distant galaxies. Images received by the cameras are divided into picture elements ("pixels," as they are called). There are 640,000 of them in the wide-field camera and about a third as many in the faint-object camera. The intensity of the light on each pixel is sent by radio to Earth as a series of electric pulses. The receiver that picks up these pulses sends them through a machine that changes them into a picture. The action is much the same as that of a TV set, which also changes electric pulses, in this case from a TV station, into pictures on the screen.

A photometer (light meter) will measure small but rapid changes in the light of an object such as a star, changes that may occur within a few thousandths of a second. Such changes will enable Space Telescope to give information about stars that are exploding, and also about pulsars— stars that pulsate and that may be stages in the collapse of many kinds of stars.

Two of the instruments are spectrographs, instruments for breaking light apart into its various wavelengths, or colors. One of them will see objects a thousand times dimmer than those observed by earlier and less powerful spacecraft. Both will enable astronomers to analyze the atmospheres of planets and also the gases of comets. In particular, Space Telescope will look for deuterium in comets. A theory about how the universe was formed states that one of the substances made at the very beginning was deuterium. Should these atoms exist in the amount expected, there would be strong proof that the theory is correct.

Later on instruments now being developed, which are sensitive to infrared (heat) energy, will be put aboard Space Telescope. They will analyze the heat energy Space Telescope receives and so provide another way of measuring the energy given off by distant stars, gas clouds, and perhaps even clouds of solid particles.

3. Placing Space Telescope in Orbit and Keeping It There

The space shuttle has proved itself through a series of successful flights, beginning with the first on April 12, 1981. Shuttles have put several satellites into orbit, completed the Spacelab operation, and shown over and over that they can perform delicate operations in space. When all is ready, Space Telescope will be stored aboard a shuttle, fitting easily into the cargo bay, which is 4.5 meters (15 feet) wide and 18 meters (60 feet) long. The weight of Space Telescope, 12,900 kilograms (28,380 pounds), is well below the 29,250 kilograms (64,000 pounds) that is the most the shuttle can carry.

Fuel that is saved by not carrying a full payload will be used to put Space Telescope into the high orbit needed to get above the effects of our atmosphere.

As mentioned earlier, the orbiter will go into orbit at an altitude of 375 miles (600 kilometers). Once it is there the cargo arm, which can reach almost to the end of the cargo bay, will be turned on. Before the launch the arm was attached to the telescope. Now it will lift the instrument free of the bay walls and swing it out beyond the cargo bay doors, which are hinged on each side.

After the astronauts have checked the telescope systems to be sure they are working properly, and after the systems have been checked by ground stations, Space Telescope will be released from the cargo arm. It will be in the same orbit as the orbiter is.

When a spaceship is in orbit, everything in the ship is also in orbit, following the same path. If you put a cup, or anything else, outside the ship, the cup would be in the same orbit going around the Earth. That's the way it will be with Space Telescope. When put outside the orbiter, it will be in orbit. To move the orbiter a small distance away from the telescope, small thruster engines will be fired. Space Telescope will be on its own: It will be in its own orbit and it will stay there for a good many years. The telescope will be free, complete with its own electricity provided by the panels of solar cells.

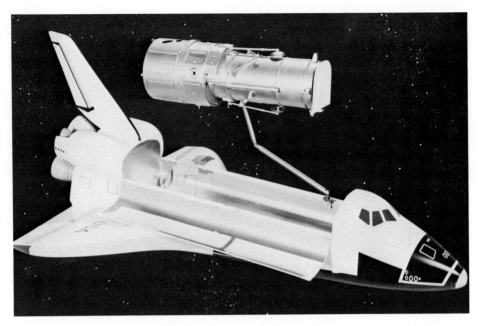

The cargo arm of orbiter lifts Space Telescope away
from the cargo bay. The instrument is then
released, solar panels expand, and Space Telescope
flies in its own orbit.

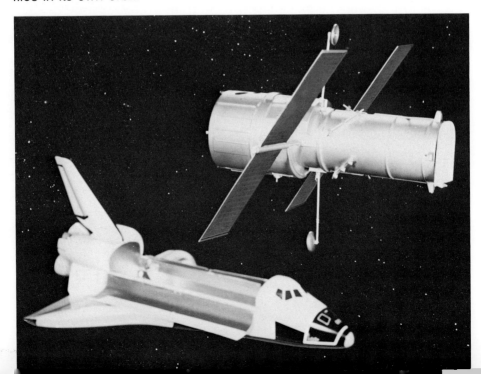

Maintenance of Space Telescope

Space dust and meteoroids may erode Space Telescope, and parts may also break down. Should this happen, future orbiters will move in close to the telescope. Once an orbiter is alongside, the solar panels will be retracted—folded up so they are out of the way. The cargo arm will reach out to the telescope, lock fast to it, and ease the instrument into the cargo bay, where it will be placed upright on a platform.

Astronauts, two at a time, will get into space suits and move from the command section of the orbiter into the cargo bay. They will move along tethers attached to the cargo area. When they reach the telescope, the astronauts will use handholds or rails and foot platforms to move up and down the telescope. Foot restraints will enable the astronauts to steady themselves so that they can pull open the hatches of the telescope. The astronauts will then be able to reach the science instruments, the optical system, and other parts. They will be able to snap out modules that need repair or updating. New devices such as the infrared analyzer will be put in place.

Without handholds and foot restraints, astronauts would not be able to make repairs. When you use a wrench in space, the bolt doesn't turn—you do. Because you are not fastened to anything, there's nothing to stop you from turning. In order to make the bolt turn, you must be anchored. That's

what the handholds and foot restraints do.

Over a period of several years, the altitude of Space Telescope may have decreased slightly. If so, once it is in the cargo bay of the orbiter, the shuttle will fire jets to take the telescope back to the original location. Once there, and after all repairs are made, the telescope will be lifted free of the orbiter, released, and sent on its way to continue making observations.

After years of operation, Space Telescope may need major repairs. For example, the metal film on the mirror may have eroded and so need replacing. Should this be so, Space Telescope will be retrieved and locked lengthwise into the cargo bay. The cargo doors will be closed over it, and the orbiter will bring the telescope back to Earth. After repairs are made, another shuttle flight will lift the telescope back into space.

Regular maintenance in space and occasional returns to Earth should keep Space Telescope operating well into the twenty-first century.

During maintenance of Space Telescope astronauts will move into the cargo bay. Here are F. Story Musgrave and Donald H. Peterson in the cargo area of Challenger during its flight in April 1983.

Before the astronauts start work, Space Telescope will be recovered and placed upright on a platform in the cargo bay.

41

4. Satellites and the Space Telescope Institute

Information gathered by the science instruments will be radioed to Earth, but not directly. It will be sent to the Tracking and Data Relay System, which is made up of two satellites stationed 35,680 kilometers (22,300 miles) above Earth. At that altitude each satellite remains above the same Earth location. The time required for the satellite to make one turn around Earth is the same as the time Earth requires to make one rotation. For example, if the satellite happened to be directly above Denver, it would always be at that location. It's as though there were an actual connection between Earth and the satellite.

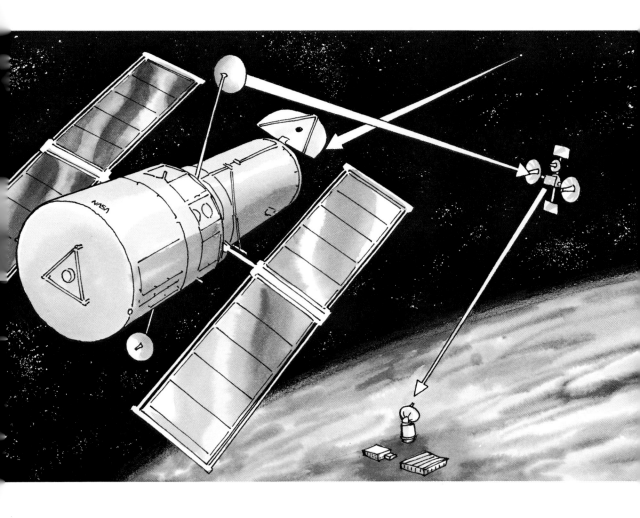

Instruments aboard Space Telescope change light to electric pulses, and these are sent to the Tracking and Data Relay Satellite. From there the information will be sent to receivers at White Sands, New Mexico, then relayed to Goddard Space Flight Center and on to the Space Telescope Institute.

These relay satellites send the data to a receiving station, a large radio antenna, located at White Sands, New Mexico. That station then sends the information back to space, and it is relayed by way of a regular commercial satellite (the kind that sends television programs) to Goddard Space Flight Center in Maryland, just outside Washington, D.C.

Goddard is not equipped to handle the data. A good many astronomers with special equipment are needed. In order to make the best use of the information, a Space Telescope Science Institute had to be set up. It is located at Johns Hopkins University in Baltimore. Some people are calling it the "World Capital of Astronomy" because astronomers around the world will be looking to Baltimore for news about the exciting discoveries made by Space Telescope.

A staff of two hundred persons at the institute, including thirty-five scientists, will analyze the information and decide on additional jobs for the telescope. There will be scientists from many different countries. In fact, 15 percent of the observing time will be used by members of the ESA, the European Space Agency. This group supplied the solar panels for the telescope, as well as the faint-object camera.

In the next chapter we'll take a look at what Space Telescope will see and send by radio to the Space Telescope Science Institute. And we'll also explore what the images may tell us about the universe.

5. Old and New Discoveries

You could say that the Space Age began when Sputnik, the first artificial satellite, was put into orbit by the Soviet Union on October 4, 1957. Since that day, more than three thousand satellites have been launched by the United States, the Soviet Union, Japan, and a few other countries. Some of them were equipped with astronomical instruments, small optical telescopes, and X ray, infrared, and ultraviolet detectors. Using those space instruments, as well as equipment mounted on Earth, scientists have made major discoveries since 1957. Those discoveries have raised a good many questions, some of which Space Telescope may answer.

What and Why Are Quasars? Quasars are quasi stars— "quasi" means "resembling." It's a good name because these are objects that look like stars. Yet they really cannot be, for they give off too much energy. Some quasars give off billions of times the energy released by the sun.

They appear to be moving at very high speeds, some at almost the speed of light, which is some 300,000 kilometers (186,000 miles) a second. To go that fast, an object must be at the edge of the universe as we are seeing it—that's some 13 billion light years away. Could quasars be that far from us?

What Are Pulsars? Pulsars are small stars, often called neutron stars, that pulsate very rapidly and give off radio waves. One of them is located in the Crab Nebula, a mass of gases expanding rapidly from a central star that exploded several thousand years ago. Pulsars may be the part of a star that remains after the star has exploded and blown away most of the gases of which it was made. These pulsating stars may be a stage that many stars go through. Presently it is believed that all stars come and go: They are born, go through a period of activity, and then die.

Space Telescope will make it possible to check this theory. Who knows: It may make new discoveries about these remains of stars that once gave off light in steady brilliance.

In 1968 a pulsar (neutron star) was found in this formation. It is the Crab Nebula located in the winter constellation of Taurus. Space Telescope will survey this area to learn more about this neutron star.

What Are Black Holes?   Black holes were discovered in the 1970s, but they had been imagined way back in the 1930s. In 1971 one was located as a companion of a star called Cygnus X–1, a star in the constellation Cygnus (the Swan). Black holes may be what large stars become as their life cycles spin out. They are concentrations of matter so dense that they exert tremendous gravitational force. The force allows nothing to escape from the mass, not even light or radio waves. We know a black hole exists near Cygnus X–1 because the gravitation of the massive black hole holds this companion star in orbit around it.

Black holes may be very common in the universe. There may be lots of them toward the center of our own galaxy, and untold numbers in other galaxies.

Space Telescope will be so accurate it will be able to detect very slight movements in a star. It may find that large numbers of them have companions that could very well be black holes.

Astronomy of the Sun

The sun is our nearest star, and so it is the one we can study in greatest detail. It has been shining for some 5 billion years and is expected to keep supplying us with energy for the next 5 billion years. Should the intensity of the sun change

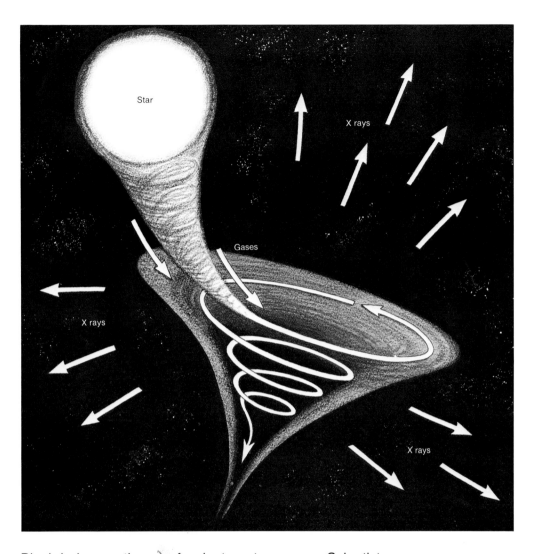

Black holes continue to fascinate astronomers. Scientists
can locate them by the X rays given off just before gases
pulled from a neighbor star are swallowed into the black
hole.

only slightly, effects on Earth would be disastrous. A slight warming of the sun would burn up all life on Earth, and a slight cooling would freeze Earth solid. Temperature changes could be caused by slight changes in the size of the sun, or they may be signaled by such changes. So astronomers want very much to learn if the sun is shrinking, as many believe it is. Space Telescope will look at other stars like the sun to see if slight size changes are occurring. If they are, that may mean the sun will soon begin to change or has already changed somewhat in size.

Astronomy of Stars and Galaxies

We are located in the Milky Way Galaxy, a huge disk-shaped formation of some 200 billion stars. It is so large that light takes 100,000 years to go across it. We are about 30,000 light-years from the center, meaning that light from the center takes 30,000 years to reach us. We are a tiny speck in the galaxy, but our instruments have enabled us to learn a lot about it. Even so, there are a good many parts of it that have not been observed by any kind of telescope.

Space Telescope will look into the center of the galaxy. Eventually it will be able to pick up infrared radiation, which appears to be very strong in that region. By studying the energy, astronomers may get a better idea of what is going

We are in the Milky Way galaxy at the location shown by
the small circle. That's some 30,000 light years from the
center.

on there. Does it mean that there are companions of vast numbers of black holes at the galactic center? Some astronomers think so.

Other galaxies will also be explored by Space Telescope to determine more accurately the amount of energy they give off, and so get an idea of what is happening to the stars of which they are made.

As you can see from the diagram on page 9, Space Telescope will see far into the infrared. Bright objects that existed long ago have cooled so they no longer produce visible light. However, they still give off infrared energy. By collecting that energy, the telescope will eventually reveal objects that are very old and events that occurred early in the history of the universe. Are quasars among such objects? How can they generate so much energy? How did planets come into existence?

Size of the Universe is related to age. The speed of light enables us to measure distance. Light goes 300,000 kilometers (186,000 miles) in one second. Therefore, if light from an object takes one second to reach us, the object must be 300,000 kilometers (186,000 miles) away. Should the light take 10 seconds to reach us, the distance to the object must be 3,000,000 kilometers (1,860,000 miles). If it takes one year to reach us, the distance to the object would be nearly 9,500,000,000,000 kilometers (6,000,000,000,000 miles)—one light-year; a light-year is the distance light travels in one year.

Many scientists believe in a theory that says the universe began some 13 to 15 billion years ago. They can pick up light from objects about 13 billion light-years away. The light has been traveling 13 billion years, so the objects producing it must have been created 13 billion years ago.

Since there are nearly 9.5 trillion kilometers (6 trillion miles) in a light-year, the radius of the universe in miles would be about 13 billion times 6 trillion miles—a number that is hard, if not impossible, to comprehend.

These scientists say everything began with a superatom that contained all the matter of the universe. When the atom exploded, the outermost matter expanded at close to the speed of light and has been doing so ever since. Since we can detect light from objects some 13 billion light-years away, we can be quite sure the event occurred 13 billion years ago. It may have happened earlier. Space Telescope may reveal clues to objects even more distant, and therefore older. The universe may be older and larger than suspected.

Another exciting possibility is that we may determine the mass of the universe, and so be able to predict what will eventually happen to the universe. Will it get bigger and bigger, or will it shrink? No one has the answer. Right now it is getting bigger, it is expanding, and it seems that the expansion will continue forever. But that possibility is far from certain. If there is more mass than has been detected, the universe may eventually collapse. The greater mass would exert enough gravity to pull the universe together. Eventually the universe may stop expanding, and it may then collapse. After billions of years the mass of the universe may once more be contained in a superatom. Once again there may be a great explosion. Space Telescope may provide clues that will indicate there is sufficient mass in the universe for this to happen.

Far-off galaxies seem to have exploded sometime in the distant past. Space Telescope will attempt to find out what happened to them. Probably disastrous changes occurred throughout those galaxies. They may have been great enough to have altered mightily any planets that may have existed in those galaxies. Could such a series of events occur eventually in our own galaxy? It is something astronomers would like to know about.

Other Planets   far out in our galaxy may be discovered by Space Telescope.

Space Telescope will be able to see and measure exactly the slightest changes in the positions of stars. These could mean that planets are in orbit around the stars. The planets would pull the stars slightly to one side and then the other as they moved around them.

Astronomers on some far-off world looking at the sun

would see it move from side to side, pulled just a bit by Jupiter's gravitation. Such movements, small as they would be, could be detected by the instruments aboard Space Telescope. We may not be able to see such planets because they are not bright enough (planets do not produce light of their own—they reflect the light of the nearby star that serves as their sun). But motions of the star would be good evidence that the planets exist. Space Telescope will be able to see star motions that have so far escaped our view.

That step would place us a lot closer to finding out if intelligent life exists on those planets that are causing the side-to-side motions, worlds located far beyond the solar system. Presently we are exploring space, looking for planets. But we really don't know where to look. Whenever a star that moves from side to side is found, we'll concentrate on that section of the sky.

6. Beyond Space Telescope

Spectacular discoveries have been made since the Space Age began in 1957 that were not even suspected before then: the thousands of rings that surround Saturn, the active volcanoes on Jupiter's satellite Io, the river beds of Mars, the high temperature of Venus, black holes, quasars, and many more. Equally spectacular discoveries will be made by Space Telescope. Some of them are anticipated. But there will be many that no one has even dreamed about.

Already scientists are thinking of new instruments for Space Telescope, and also larger telescopes. The next generation of space shuttles will be larger, so they will be able to carry larger loads. The new telescopes will be improved versions of Space Telescope. To make them easier to maintain,

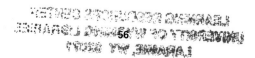

In the years ahead larger versions of the shuttle
will carry sensitive infrared telescopes into orbit.
They will detect faint sources of infrared radiation.

Eventually a very large reflector telescope will
be in orbit, as shown at the right. It will be attached
to a laboratory-observatory that will be serviced by
astronauts aboard orbiters.

they will probably be mounted on platforms in space, carried there by shuttles and erected in space by astronauts. A still larger supertelescope may be built into the casing of the main fuel tank of the shuttle. The tank may be carried into orbit, where it would provide the framework for the telescope.

Following these stages, there will be telescopes so large they must be carried into orbit piece by piece and assembled in space. The new generation of telescopes will be so powerful that an instrument in California could see clearly a small sparrow in the skies over Boston, and perhaps even the separate feathers.

The new generation of telescopes will reveal the universe as never seen before. They may detect other planets going around distant stars, as mentioned earlier. They may even see signs of civilizations that are flourishing out there, just as our civilization flourishes on this planet. That would be the greatest discovery ever made by Earth people.

Index

Index

air blanket, 7
astronauts, 39, *41*
astronomy
  ancient, 1
  of galaxies and stars, 50–52
  Galileo's contributions to, 1–2,
    2, *3*, 11, *11*, 12, 15
  of sun, 48–50
atmosphere, 5–10
  "windows" in, 7, *8*

baffles, stray-light, *14*, 22, *23*, 31
batteries, solar, *24*, 30, 31, 33
binoculars, 15, *16*
black holes, 48, *49*, 52, 56
brightness of stars, *16*, 17

cameras, in Space Telescope, 5, 14, 34
cargo arm, 25, 37, *38*
cargo bay, 3–5, 25, 36, 41

Cassegrain, Guillaume, *11*, 14
charge controller, *24*
color fringes, 12–13, *13*
communication system, *24*, 30, 32, 33,
  42–44
computers, *24*, 32
Crab Nebula, 46, *47*
Cygnus X-1, 48

deuterium, 35
digital interface unit, *24*
Dione, *6*

Earth
  magnetic field of, 31
  rotation of, 42
  telescopes located on, *viii*, 5, 8–10,
    17, 18
electrical power, *19*, 20–22, 30, 33, 37,
  38, 44